Check-in & Color

A COLORING BOOK & GRATITUDE JOURNAL FOR SCHOOL NUTRITION PROFESSIONALS

Shannon Ebron, MS, RDN, LD

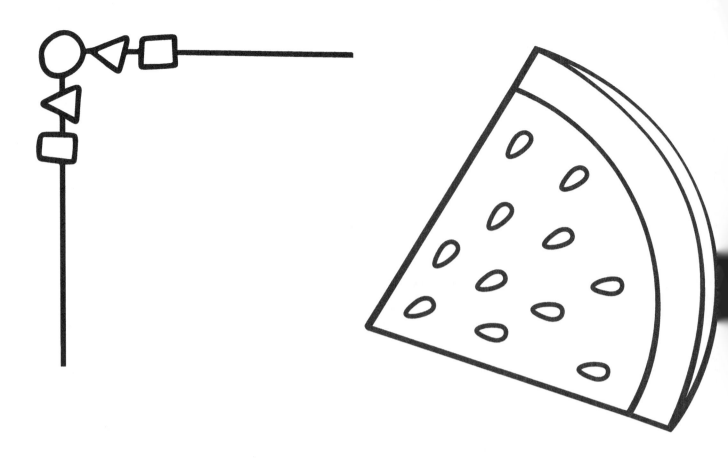

Check-in & Color: A Coloring Book & Gratitude Journal for School Nutrition Professionals
Copyright © 2022 Shannon Ebron, MS, RDN, LD

ISBN: 979-8-9872735-0-0

Cover and Interior Design: Author
Images: Canva Pro.

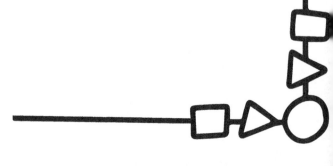

This Activity Book Belongs To:

_____

This page is intentionally left blank.

Hey, Friend!

Did you ever dream you would put meals on a bus, serve meals curbside, or make food kits containing a week of school meals and snacks? Me either, but we did it! The commitment shown by School Nutrition Professionals to make sure students have delicious meals has been astounding! In this pandemic, each day brings a new challenge to us in the cafeteria, warehouse, central office, or school garden and we have rolled with the punches; stepping up to keep children healthy and ready to learn. Now it is time to focus on you!

I created *Check-in & Color* to give yourself time to relax, reflect, and laugh! Color pages sprinkled with things you hear in the school cafeteria, repetitive things you say, tools you use and rules you follow as a School Nutrition Professional.

Whatever role you serve in nourishing children, school nutrition professionals change the world one meal at a time. I hope this activity book celebrates you and helps you to focus on the good things in life.

Enjoy!

Shannon Ebron

This page is intentionally left blank.

This page is intentionally left blank.

Gratitude Check

Date: ....

I am grateful for my family because... ———————————————

———————————————————————————————

Something good that happened to me today... ———————————

———————————————————————————————

I am grateful for my coworkers/friendship with...because ————————

———————————————————————————————

I am grateful for who I am because... ———————————————

———————————————————————————————

Something funny, cute, nice, etc. a student did that I am grateful for...

———————————————————————————————

Something else I am grateful for... ————————————————

———————————————————————————————

△▽▷△ △▽△▷△▽▷△ △▽△▽△▷▷△ △▽△▽△

This page is intentionally left blank.

☺

This page is intentionally left blank.

Gratitude Check

Date: ....

I am grateful for my family because... ————————————

————————————————————————————

Something good that happened to me today... ——————————

————————————————————————————

I am grateful for my coworkers/friendship with...because ————

————————————————————————————

I am grateful for who I am because... ——————————————

————————————————————————————

Something funny, cute, nice, etc. a student did that I am grateful for...

————————————————————————————

Something else I am grateful for... ——————————————

————————————————————————————

△▽▷△ △▽△▽△▷△ △▽△▽△▷△ △▽△▽△

☺

This page is intentionally left blank.

This page is intentionally left blank.

Gratitude Check

Date: ....

I am grateful for my family because... _____

_____

Something good that happened to me today... _____

_____

I am grateful for my coworkers/friendship with...because _____

_____

I am grateful for who I am because... _____

_____

Something funny, cute, nice, etc. a student did that I am grateful for...

_____

Something else I am grateful for... _____

_____

△▽▽△ △▽△▽△▽▽△ △▽△▽△▽▽△ △▽△▽△

This page is intentionally left blank.

This page is intentionally left blank.

Gratitude Check

Date: ....

I am grateful for my family because... ————————————————

————————————————————————————

Something good that happened to me today... ——————————

————————————————————————————

I am grateful for my coworkers/friendship with...because ————————

————————————————————————————

I am grateful for who I am because... ——————————————

————————————————————————————

Something funny, cute, nice, etc. a student did that I am grateful for...

————————————————————————————

Something else I am grateful for... ————————————————

————————————————————————————

△▽▷▷△ △▽△▽△▷▷△ △▽△▽△▷▷△ △▽△▽△

This page is intentionally left blank.

My love for students is beyond measure

This page is intentionally left blank.

Gratitude Check

Date: ....

I am grateful for my family because... _____

_____

Something good that happened to me today... _____

_____

I am grateful for my coworkers/friendship with...because _____

_____

I am grateful for who I am because... _____

_____

Something funny, cute, nice, etc. a student did that I am grateful for...

_____

Something else I am grateful for... _____

_____

△▽▷△ △▽△▽△▷▷△ △▽△▽△▷▷△ △▽△▽△

This page is intentionally left blank.

This page is intentionally left blank.

Gratitude Check

Date: ....

I am grateful for my family because... _____

_____

Something good that happened to me today... _____

_____

I am grateful for my coworkers/friendship with...because _____

_____

I am grateful for who I am because... _____

_____

Something funny, cute, nice, etc. a student did that I am grateful for...

_____

Something else I am grateful for... _____

_____

◁▽▷▷◁ ◁▽◁▽◁▷▷◁ ◁▽◁▽◁▷▷◁ ◁▽◁▽◁

This page is intentionally left blank.

This page is intentionally left blank.

Gratitude Check

Date: ....

I am grateful for my family because... ―――――――――――――――

_____

Something good that happened to me today... ―――――――――――

_____

I am grateful for my coworkers/friendship with...because ―――――――

_____

I am grateful for who I am because... ―――――――――――――――

_____

Something funny, cute, nice, etc. a student did that I am grateful for...

_____

Something else I am grateful for... ―――――――――――――――

_____

△▽▷▷△ △▽△▽△▷▷△ △▽△▽△▷▷△ △▽△▽△

This page is intentionally left blank.

When the lunch lady slides you an extra chicken nugget

This page is intentionally left blank.

Gratitude Check

Date: ....

I am grateful for my family because... _____

_____

Something good that happened to me today... _____

_____

I am grateful for my coworkers/friendship with...because _____

_____

I am grateful for who I am because... _____

_____

Something funny, cute, nice, etc. a student did that I am grateful for...

_____

Something else I am grateful for... _____

_____

◁▷▷◁ ◁▷◁▷◁▷▷◁ ◁▷◁▷◁▷▷◁ ◁▷◁▷◁

This page is intentionally left blank.

☺

This page is intentionally left blank.

Gratitude Check

Date: ....

I am grateful for my family because... —————————————————

————————————————————————————————————

Something good that happened to me today... ————————————

————————————————————————————————————

I am grateful for my coworkers/friendship with...because ————————

————————————————————————————————————

I am grateful for who I am because... ———————————————

————————————————————————————————————

Something funny, cute, nice, etc. a student did that I am grateful for...

————————————————————————————————————

Something else I am grateful for... ———————————————

————————————————————————————————————

△▽△▽△ △▽△▽△▽▷△ △▽△▽△▷▷△ △▽△▽△

This page is intentionally left blank.

This or That?

CIRCLE YOUR ANSWER.

Child Nutrition	School Nutrition
Reach-in Cooler	Milk Box
Smock	Apron
Central Kitchen	Conventional Kitchen
Breakfast in Class	Breakfast After Bell
Offer	Serve
SSO	SFSP
School Food Dude	Lunch Lady
Recess First	Lunch First
Scratch Cooking	Heat & Serve

This page is intentionally left blank.

Gratitude Check

Date: ....

I am grateful for my family because... ————————————

————————————————————————————

Something good that happened to me today... ————————

————————————————————————————

I am grateful for my coworkers/friendship with...because ————

————————————————————————————

I am grateful for who I am because... ————————————

————————————————————————————

Something funny, cute, nice, etc. a student did that I am grateful for...

————————————————————————————

Something else I am grateful for... ————————————

————————————————————————————

◁▽▷◁ ▷◁▽◁▷◁▷◁ ▷◁▽◁▽◁▷◁ ▷◁▽◁▽◁

☺
This page is intentionally left blank.

Color the scoop handle to match the scoop size.

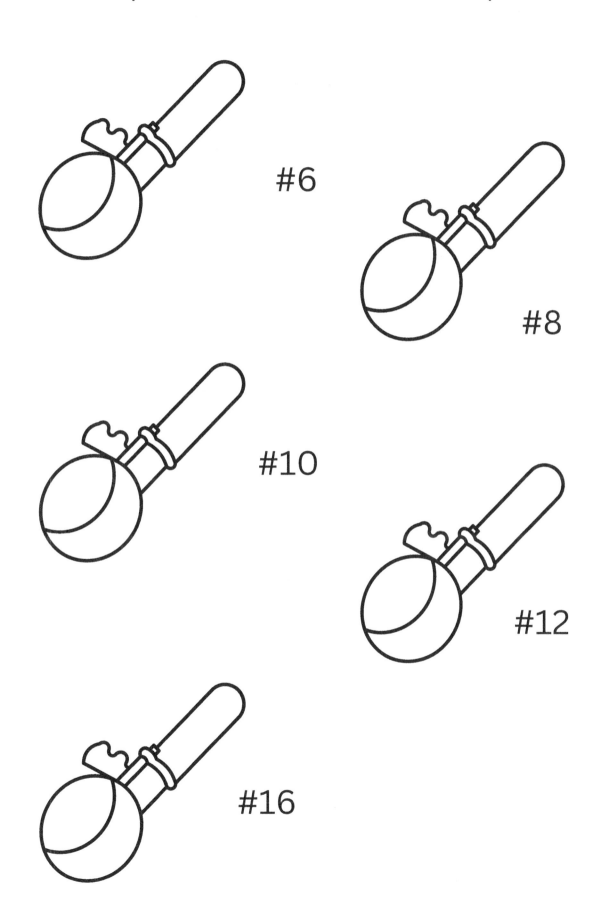

#6

#8

#10

#12

#16

This page is intentionally left blank.

Gratitude Check

Date: ....

I am grateful for my family because... _____

_____

Something good that happened to me today... _____

_____

I am grateful for my coworkers/friendship with...because _____

_____

I am grateful for who I am because... _____

_____

Something funny, cute, nice, etc. a student did that I am grateful for...

_____

Something else I am grateful for... _____

_____

△▽▷△ △▽△▽△▷△ △▽△▽△▷△ △▽△▽△

This page is intentionally left blank.

Color the scoop handle to match the scoop size.

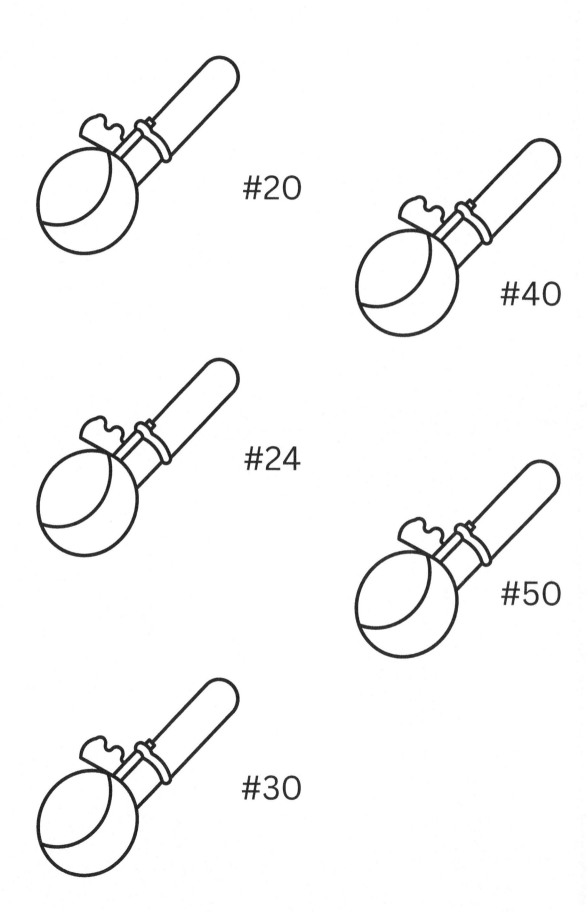

#20

#40

#24

#50

#30

This page is intentionally left blank.

Gratitude Check

Date: ....

I am grateful for my family because... _____

_____

Something good that happened to me today... _____

_____

I am grateful for my coworkers/friendship with...because _____

_____

I am grateful for who I am because... _____

_____

Something funny, cute, nice, etc. a student did that I am grateful for...

_____

Something else I am grateful for... _____

_____

This page is intentionally left blank.

Nobody:

Lunch Lady:

Make sure you grab a fruit or vegetable

☺
This page is intentionally left blank.

Gratitude Check

Date: ....

I am grateful for my family because... ——————————————

———————————————————————————————

Something good that happened to me today... ————————————

———————————————————————————————

I am grateful for my coworkers/friendship with...because ——————

———————————————————————————————

I am grateful for who I am because... ——————————————

———————————————————————————————

Something funny, cute, nice, etc. a student did that I am grateful for...

———————————————————————————————

Something else I am grateful for... ———————————————

———————————————————————————————

△▽▷△ △▽△▽△▷▷△ △▽△▽△▷▷△ △▽△▽△

This page is intentionally left blank.

Meat

Meat Alternates

This page is intentionally left blank.

Gratitude Check

Date: ....

I am grateful for my family because... ————————————

_____

Something good that happened to me today... ——————————

_____

I am grateful for my coworkers/friendship with...because ————

_____

I am grateful for who I am because... ——————————————

_____

Something funny, cute, nice, etc. a student did that I am grateful for...

_____

Something else I am grateful for... ——————————————

_____

△▽▷▷△ △▽△▽△▷▷△ △▽△▽△▷▷△ △▽△▽△

SCHOOL FOOD
DUDES
ARE ONE IN A MELON

This page is intentionally left blank.

Gratitude Check

Date: ....

I am grateful for my family because... ———————————

_____

Something good that happened to me today... ——————————

_____

I am grateful for my coworkers/friendship with...because ——————

_____

I am grateful for who I am because... ——————————————

_____

Something funny, cute, nice, etc. a student did that I am grateful for...

_____

Something else I am grateful for... ——————————————

_____

△▽▷△ △▽△▽△▷▷△ △▽△▽△▷▷△ △▽△▽△

This page is intentionally left blank.

This or That?

CIRCLE YOUR ANSWER.

Chocolate Milk	Strawberry Milk
Corn Dog	Hot Dog
3-Compartment Sink	Dish Machine
School Breakfast	School Lunch
A La Carte	Reimbursable Meal
Spring Break	Winter Break
Hat	Hairnet
Spicy Chicken Sandwich	Chicken Sandwich
Cook	Cashier
Elementary School	Secondary School

This page is intentionally left blank.

Gratitude Check

Date: ....

I am grateful for my family because... ⸻⸻⸻⸻

⸻⸻⸻⸻⸻⸻⸻⸻⸻

Something good that happened to me today... ⸻⸻⸻

⸻⸻⸻⸻⸻⸻⸻⸻⸻

I am grateful for my coworkers/friendship with...because ⸻⸻

⸻⸻⸻⸻⸻⸻⸻⸻⸻

I am grateful for who I am because... ⸻⸻⸻⸻

⸻⸻⸻⸻⸻⸻⸻⸻⸻

Something funny, cute, nice, etc. a student did that I am grateful for...

⸻⸻⸻⸻⸻⸻⸻⸻⸻

Something else I am grateful for... ⸻⸻⸻⸻

⸻⸻⸻⸻⸻⸻⸻⸻⸻

△▽△▷△ △▽△▽△▷△ △▽△▽△▷△ △▽△▽△

This page is intentionally left blank.

This page is intentionally left blank.

Gratitude Check

Date: ....

I am grateful for my family because... ————————————

————————————————————

Something good that happened to me today... ———————

————————————————————

I am grateful for my coworkers/friendship with...because ————

————————————————————

I am grateful for who I am because... ———————————

————————————————————

Something funny, cute, nice, etc. a student did that I am grateful for...

————————————————————

Something else I am grateful for... ———————————

————————————————————

This page is intentionally left blank.

Grains

This page is intentionally left blank.

Gratitude Check

Date: ....

I am grateful for my family because... ─────────────

─────────────────────────────

Something good that happened to me today... ──────────

─────────────────────────────

I am grateful for my coworkers/friendship with...because ─────────

─────────────────────────────

I am grateful for who I am because... ──────────────

─────────────────────────────

Something funny, cute, nice, etc. a student did that I am grateful for...

─────────────────────────────

Something else I am grateful for... ─────────────────

─────────────────────────────

△▽△▷△ △▽△▷△▽△ △▽△▷△▽△ △▽△▷△

This page is intentionally left blank.

I AM A HUNGER HEALER

This page is intentionally left blank.

Gratitude Check

Date: ....

I am grateful for my family because... _____

_____

Something good that happened to me today... _____

_____

I am grateful for my coworkers/friendship with...because _____

_____

I am grateful for who I am because... _____

_____

Something funny, cute, nice, etc. a student did that I am grateful for...

_____

Something else I am grateful for... _____

_____

△▽▷▽△ △▽△▽△▷▷△ △▽△▽△▷▷△ △▽△▽△

This page is intentionally left blank.

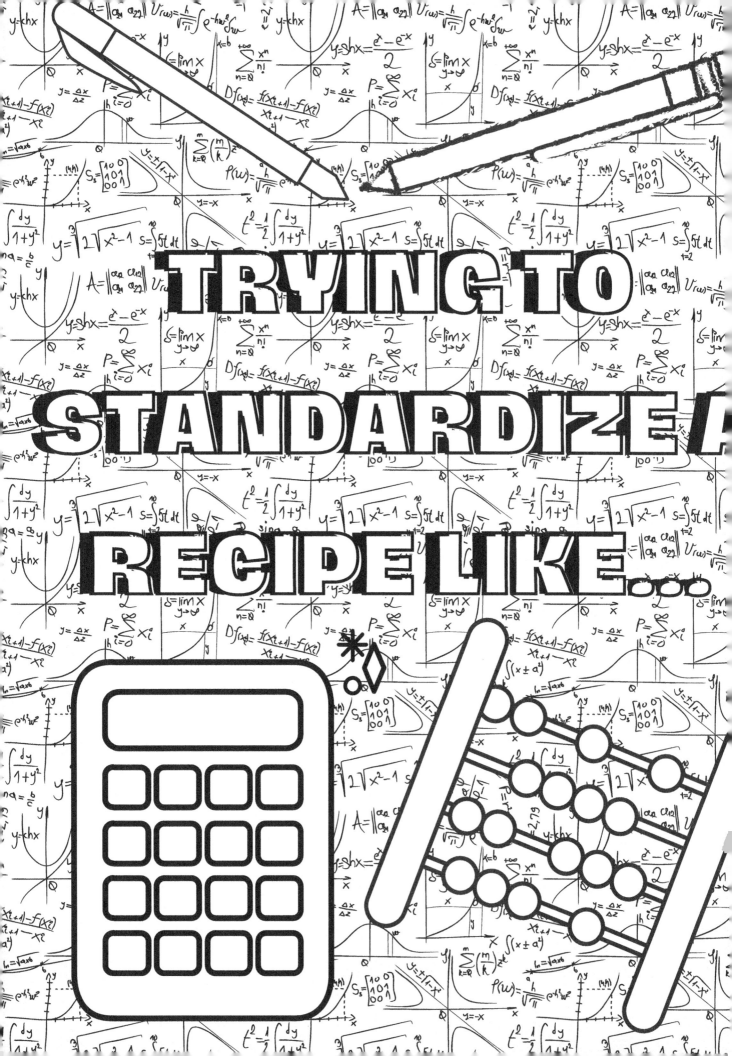

This page is intentionally left blank.

Gratitude Check

Date: ....

I am grateful for my family because... —————————————————

_____

Something good that happened to me today... ————————————

_____

I am grateful for my coworkers/friendship with...because ——————

_____

I am grateful for who I am because... ————————————————

_____

Something funny, cute, nice, etc. a student did that I am grateful for...

_____

Something else I am grateful for... ————————————————

_____

△▽▷▷△ △▽△▽△▷▷△ △▽△▽△▷▷△ △▽△▽△

This page is intentionally left blank.

This or That?

CIRCLE YOUR ANSWER.

Foam Tray	Melamine Tray
Last Day of School	First Day of School
Fruit	Vegetable
Pin Number	ID Card
Ketchup	Mustard
Menu	Cook's Choice
Snow Day	School Day
Summer Meals	Summer Vacation
Dry Storage	Cold Storage
Spoodle	Tongs

☺

This page is intentionally left blank.

Gratitude Check

Date: ....

I am grateful for my family because... ————————————————

————————————————————————————————————

Something good that happened to me today... ————————————

————————————————————————————————————

I am grateful for my coworkers/friendship with...because ————————

————————————————————————————————————

I am grateful for who I am because... ————————————————

————————————————————————————————————

Something funny, cute, nice, etc. a student did that I am grateful for...

————————————————————————————————————

Something else I am grateful for... ————————————————

————————————————————————————————————

This page is intentionally left blank.

This page is intentionally left blank.

Gratitude Check

Date: ....

I am grateful for my family because... ———————————

———————————————————

Something good that happened to me today... ——————

———————————————————

I am grateful for my coworkers/friendship with...because ———

———————————————————

I am grateful for who I am because... ————————

———————————————————

Something funny, cute, nice, etc. a student did that I am grateful for...

———————————————————

Something else I am grateful for... ————————

———————————————————

◁△▽◁▷△ △▽◁▷◁▽▷▷◁ △▽◁▷◁▽▷▷◁ △▽◁▽◁

☺

This page is intentionally left blank.

☺

This page is intentionally left blank.

Gratitude Check

Date: ....

I am grateful for my family because... ─────────────────

─────────────────────────────────

Something good that happened to me today... ───────────

─────────────────────────────────

I am grateful for my coworkers/friendship with...because ─────────

─────────────────────────────────

I am grateful for who I am because... ─────────────

─────────────────────────────────

Something funny, cute, nice, etc. a student did that I am grateful for...

─────────────────────────────────

Something else I am grateful for... ──────────────

─────────────────────────────────

△▽▷△ △▽△▽△▷△ △▽△▽△▷△ △▽△▽△

This page is intentionally left blank.

This page is intentionally left blank.

Gratitude Check

Date: ....

I am grateful for my family because... _____

_____

Something good that happened to me today... _____

_____

I am grateful for my coworkers/friendship with...because _____

_____

I am grateful for who I am because... _____

_____

Something funny, cute, nice, etc. a student did that I am grateful for...

_____

Something else I am grateful for... _____

_____

△▽▽△ △▽△▽△▽▽△ △▽△▽△▽▽△ △▽△▽△

This page is intentionally left blank.

VEGETABLES

This page is intentionally left blank.

Gratitude Check

Date: ....

I am grateful for my family because... ——————————————

_____

Something good that happened to me today... ———————————

_____

I am grateful for my coworkers/friendship with...because ——————

_____

I am grateful for who I am because... ——————————————

_____

Something funny, cute, nice, etc. a student did that I am grateful for...

_____

Something else I am grateful for... ——————————————

_____

△▽▷△▽△ △▽△▽△▷▷△ △▽△▽△▷▷△ △▽△▽△

This page is intentionally left blank.

This page is intentionally left blank.

Gratitude Check

Date: ....

I am grateful for my family because... _____

_____

Something good that happened to me today... _____

_____

I am grateful for my coworkers/friendship with...because _____

_____

I am grateful for who I am because... _____

_____

Something funny, cute, nice, etc. a student did that I am grateful for...

_____

Something else I am grateful for... _____

_____

△▽▷▷△ △▽◁▽◁▷▷△ △▽◁▽◁▷▷△ △▽◁▽◁

:)
This page is intentionally left blank.

This page is intentionally left blank.

Gratitude Check

Date: ....

I am grateful for my family because... ——————————

——————————

Something good that happened to me today... ——————

——————————

I am grateful for my coworkers/friendship with...because ————

——————————

I am grateful for who I am because... ————————

——————————

Something funny, cute, nice, etc. a student did that I am grateful for...

——————————

Something else I am grateful for... ————————

——————————

This page is intentionally left blank.

This page is intentionally left blank.

Gratitude Check

Date: ....

I am grateful for my family because... ————————————

————————————————————————

Something good that happened to me today... ——————————

————————————————————————

I am grateful for my coworkers/friendship with...because ——————

————————————————————————

I am grateful for who I am because... —————————————

————————————————————————

Something funny, cute, nice, etc. a student did that I am grateful for...

————————————————————————

Something else I am grateful for... ——————————————

————————————————————————

◁▽◁▽▷◁ ◁▽◁▽◁▷▷◁ ◁▽◁▽◁▷▷◁ ◁▽◁▽◁

This page is intentionally left blank.

This page is intentionally left blank.

Gratitude Check

Date: ....

I am grateful for my family because... ————————————————

————————————————————————————————

Something good that happened to me today... ————————————

————————————————————————————————

I am grateful for my coworkers/friendship with...because ————————

————————————————————————————————

I am grateful for who I am because... ——————————————

————————————————————————————————

Something funny, cute, nice, etc. a student did that I am grateful for...

————————————————————————————————

Something else I am grateful for... ——————————————————

————————————————————————————————

This page is intentionally left blank.

This page is intentionally left blank.

Gratitude Check

Date: ....

I am grateful for my family because... _____

_____

Something good that happened to me today... _____

_____

I am grateful for my coworkers/friendship with...because _____

_____

I am grateful for who I am because... _____

_____

Something funny, cute, nice, etc. a student did that I am grateful for...

_____

Something else I am grateful for... _____

_____

△▽△▽△ △▽△▽△▽▷△ △▽△▽△▽▷△ △▽△▽△

This page is intentionally left blank.

Bye, Friend!

...Or see you later on social media.

I hope you enjoyed this coloring book and gratitude journal made for School Nutrition Professionals. In the meantime keep being awesome!

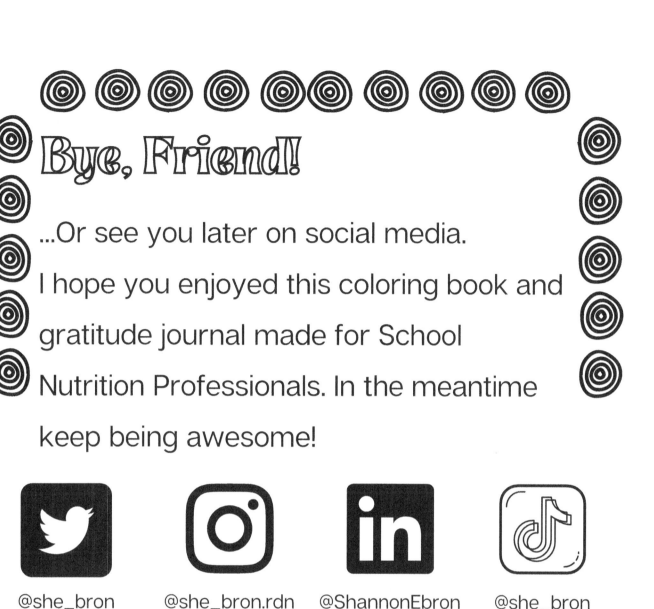

| @she_bron | @she_bron.rdn | @ShannonEbron | @she_bron |

This page is intentionally left blank.

Made in the USA
Monee, IL
17 July 2023

39279520R00090